The Art

of

Beginning

Again

Also by Sarah Cowan

Keep Me Sane

The Art

of

Beginning

Again

Sarah Cowan

THE ART OF BEGINNING AGAIN

Published by Sarah Cowan, Edmonton, Canada.
Illustrations by Grey Peterson

ISBN:
Paperback 978-1-77354-703-9
EBook 978-1-77354-704-6

Publication assistance by

PageMaster
PUBLISHING
PageMaster.ca

For those who inspired it, but will not read it.

CONTENTS

EMBRACING CHANGE 8

RESILIENCE 66

SELF-DISCOVERY 108

STARTING ANEW 152

INDEX OF TITLES 202

EMBRACING CHANGE

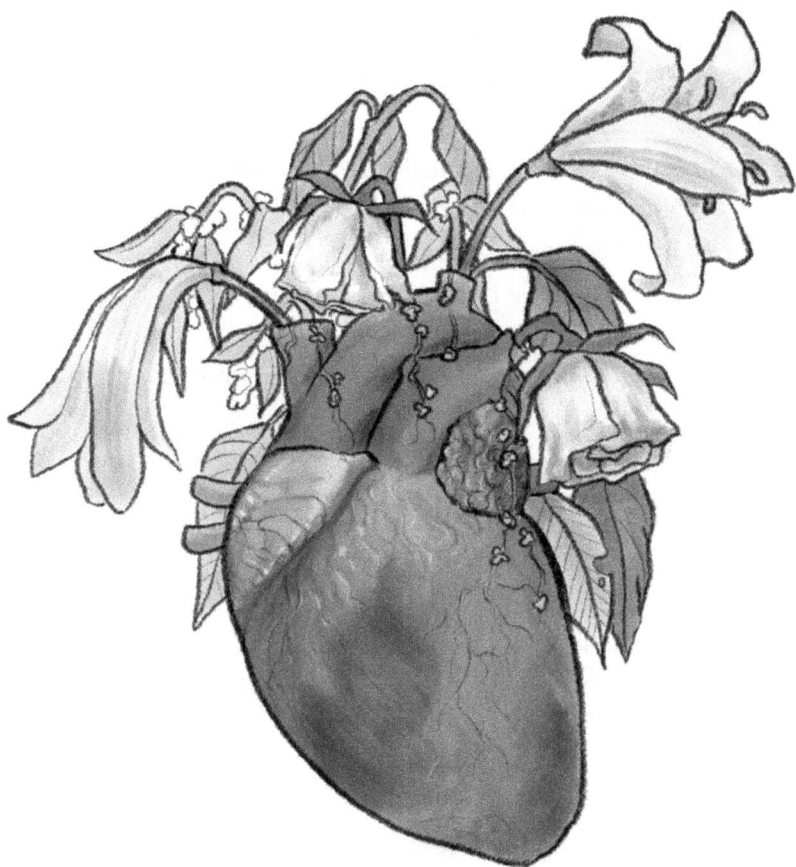

The Genesis

the beginning is such a glorious concept
first page, a fresh start
starting from square one
old book is closing and a new one is opening

a pit in your stomach flutters with butterflies
filling with anticipation on what is to come
some beginnings are clear
while some are buried amongst the
chaos and reveal themselves
after you've grown beyond your capabilities

years from now
you'll turn around
reminiscing at how far you've truly come
recognizing that same person who once was
is no longer
it is an achingly slow process
but listen when I tell you that
it is also a sensational one

at the beginning you know
you are oblivious to how it will all end
that is the joy of it

A Little Reminder

you are allowed to
tell the world what they did to you
or how they tortured you

speaking your truth
means shedding light to
their shadows

if they wanted people to
believe that they are kind
they would have done
kind things to you

Knife As Words

you are not my priority
he once told me

those words pierced me like a dagger
that should have
been the bleeding truth
screaming for me to plead for
my heart and leave sooner

but I didn't

I stayed because of love
I stayed because I wanted to fix him
I stayed because I thought maybe
just maybe
his mind would change and
I would become important to him again

those words have become
permanently etched in my brain
no matter the amount of times I try to
shake it out of my head
it will *never* leave

that pain will always live on

Lost

during sobbing nights and heartbreak
you will scream to the moon
I lost them!

but they lost you too

they lost someone who once cared for them
more than anyone has ever cared before

their nights now filled with staring at a black screen
hoping it'll light up with your name on it
your person lost someone who
always put their partner first

they may play it off and make it seem like
you don't matter or never did matter
but you do matter

they lost you just as much as you lost them

And This Is How It Is

wearing their hearts on their sleeve
people who stand before you
have already told you their
true feelings

did you see it?

if you were a priority to them
you would feel like one

you would know that they love you
even when their words didn't tell you
no questions of hesitancy
would ever come from it

how someone treats you is *exactly*
how they feel about you
don't let their words skew you astray
you could care so much about someone
and they won't even bat an eye if you walk out

and this is how it is

Paralyzed

my body is frozen
but my mind screams
at me to move

but I can't

why can't you just move?
you have so much to do
there's no time to sit
around and do nothing

Just get up.
Get up.
Get up.
Get. Up.

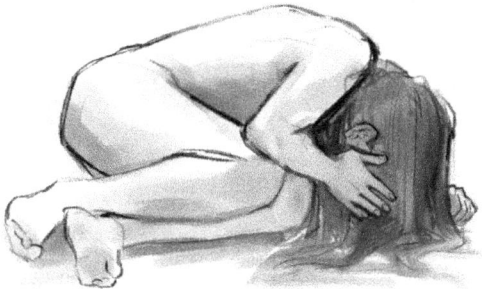

I Didn't Have A Choice

I defended you all these years
despite everything I overheard
I always told everyone that
you were the good guy in our story

I was oblivious to the truth

you taught me that I need to find
love in all the wrong places
you taught me to cower in fear the moment
a voice gets raised at me
you taught me that being
desperate for love will give me
anyone to solve my crave for attention
the attention you never gave me

it's not like I could "walk away" from you
I didn't have a choice of your presence
But you *did*

you pull me by a string
keep me far like a friend
but never anything more
even when I once longed for it
days turned to weekend visits
weekend visits turned to monthly visits
monthly visits turned into calls
which fell to texts

I didn't ask for any of this
this was all your doing

She Was Only A Kid

for once in my life
I felt sorry for myself
not my present self
but for the little me

the little girl who danced around the kitchen
offered to help her parents before any
questions ever came out
the little girl who laughed at any joke
and loved to play imaginary games

she got corrupted so soon
grew up too fast

now that bright little girl is burnt out
reality hit her before she could even blink

as she got older
men sexualized her
expectations got higher and
everything she did was labeled wrong
boys began to crush on her
while simultaneously
crushing her self esteem
treating her like she meant nothing

life showed her how harsh reality is
showing no remorse for anyone
not even a child

she was forced to grow up too fast
now all that's left is a gaping hole
inside her chest
with a little girl crying in the corner
wondering where it all went wrong

Do You Hear Me?

will you forget about me?
seems like you already have
will you love them more than me?
treating them how I longed for

will you forget about me?
watching them grow and you trying to be better
do you love them more?
maybe I'll scream it to you or write it in this letter

will you forget about me?
my childish heart yearns for someone to be so
involved
was that too much to ask for?
after twenty-three years, this problem remains
unsolved

do you hear me?
I sound like a broken record, I'm sure you'd agree
how often do you see them?
probably more than you see me

but I hope you'd disagree

Questions & Silence

do you ever think about
things you want to say to me?
I'm sorry?
I miss you?
I can't stop thinking about you?
you hurt me?
I hate you?
or maybe nothing at all?

our ending felt
incomplete
you walked away and I didn't follow

have you moved on?
is it just me stuck in the past?

my mind floods with unanswered questions
but you don't talk to me
and I can't reach out

so I guess I will make friends with the silences
and unanswered questions

Unanswered Questions

someone whom I loved dearly
turned against me
leaving me in the dust all alone

the day I walked to you planning to say
"I love you" for the first time
instead I walked away from you
with a shattered heart

then you avoided me like the plague
pushed me away while I still stared and
admired you in class
as you sat two rows over from me

still wearing the necklace you gave me for my
birthday
wearing it made me still feel
connected to you, though you
wanted nothing to do with me

I learned to heal on my own
despite all the unanswered questions

later followed complete radio silence
now we haven't talked in almost seven years
and I still have unanswered questions

Pieces Of You

I take pieces of everyone I have ever loved
and alter who I am because of them

my first relationship helped make me less anxious
taught me how to live carefree
releasing the fear that creeps in
when you live dangerously
teaching me what not to expect in a relationship
together we were only meant to fall apart
but he taught me what loving
another human could do to someone

my second partner helped me
learn to observe loved ones closely
and he taught me the value of true love
I still hold onto my gear shift when I drive because
it was something I watched him do back then
I still twirl a pencil in my hand cause I watched him
do that in english class back in high school
he taught me that true love does exist
and the importance of observing and admiring
every tiny detail in someone you love

my next lover helped me find myself
from meeting him when I was already
kicked down in my lowest, he lifted me back up
made me realize that I don't need
to change myself to appease someone else
that it is possible for someone to love
me exactly as I am
making the confident and strong
woman who stands before you
he has helped me build myself
to who I should've been long ago
I've focused on myself and built me for me
not for anyone else
he has taught me that true love does exist

no matter who I have loved in the past
they all permanently alter who I am
big or small adjustments
together for a long time or a short time
they had a massive impact on me to this day
and I am eternally grateful to have evidence
of these past loves.

Words

the silence is screaming at me
his silence
her silence

he left me in silence yet still lives on
she left me in silence but is dead
I want answers from them
I want words
don't ask me what kind of words
reassuring ones
right?
anything?
maybe

but I get no words
from anyone
just hurt

Not Love

when you feel
unseen
unheard
unwanted
is when you know you're growing
something that isn't love.

you never want to admit that it's over
so you'll fight and put up with the constant
arguments
hoping that "tomorrow will be better"
hearing from them won't spark joy anymore
no text or call could bring back those butterflies
like from when you were kids just
exploring the beginning of something new

maybe you fell in love with them because of
their charming personality
now their extroverted tendencies get under your
skin
never seeing them and never
feeling like you were a priority
or maybe you felt like you never were one

love is not love when you know in your heart
something is just not right

He Loves Me, He Loves Me Not

he loves me
after he said he couldn't make it
to the school play I invited him to
he came unexpectedly
then after we went for a drive and
I swear it was the night we fell in love

he loves me not
I was told from a friend who
talked to you that you dating me
was all an experiment that failed
is that all I was to you?
an *experiment*?

he loves me
gifting me a sterling silver necklace for my birthday
then asking me to be his girlfriend

he loves me not
he said he shouldn't be my priority
but how can I not prioritize someone
who meant so much to me?

he loves me
giving me butterflies and going out of his way to
see me
even if it's for five minutes and he's really busy

Sarah Cowan

he loves me not
"you are not my priority" he told me after
I said I never feel like we get to spend time together

he loves me
giving me a new year's kiss
seeing that genuine smile
creating fireworks within us

he loves me not
I felt like I was on my knees
begging for more time
and love from him
after all, I was the one who said yes

I guess he loved me not
all this just for him to pull away
while leaving me broken and alone

Not As Planned

tightness in my chest
what happened?
my plans changed
but why would they do that?
this isn't what I planned to happen

why is an elephant sitting on my chest?
I feel a sense of panic creep on me
knowing that I never had a plan b
what am I to do next?
I should've made a plan b

Blindside

"we never saw that coming,"
they say,
"she was dying right in front of us"

how can you not see it coming?
she gave you all these signs that you chose to ignore

ignoring calls and texts,
avoiding eye contact,
losing her bubbly personality
while masking it with someone who isn't her

they'll say they've been blindsided
but she thinks they were being blinded
by their own versions of her

she's easy to read
only if you read the fine print

When Change Comes

I will greet change at the door
staring blankly, wondering what to say
"are you right for me?"
"are you at the right house?"

but change will let itself in
without permission, without warning

when change comes
I will not fear
change will bring in all of their baggage

but I will make room

I will allow change to build a home
with me
resisting change and this new
sense of normal will only make it worse

I will greet change with open arms
and a selfless smile

"come on in, I've been waiting for you."

Impending Doom

I can't describe what I'm feeling
a panicked sense of what is next
constantly worried on what will happen
worried how anything can rip me apart
in the matter of seconds

impending doom
but none of it is true
it's all in my head

everything is okay
I remind myself
this is all just your brain telling you
nasty little things to make you think this way

right?

Rainbow Bridge

I never stop thinking of the moment you fell asleep
on that bed before you passed on
the family was crying and I'd already gone numb

"I can't cry. I need to be strong for her." I told
myself walking into the clinic, you in my arms
while you laid on that bed I stayed at your side
looking you directly in the eye

"I'm going to be the last thing you see before
you go to heaven" I told myself
I'm going to be strong and not cry
so that way she stays calm

every so often she'd lift her head
getting confirmation that everyone else is still there
then she went back to staring straight back at me
and I didn't *dare* to look away

I only looked away once her eyes closed and
that dreaded needle took her away from me
I watched as she went into her eternal sleep

only *then*

after she has gone to sleep and not able to see me
was when I broke
when she finally passed away
I collapsed on the table that has held me up
and sobbed

cried that my best friend is truly gone
that my childhood dog I grew up with for all my life
is now only a memory
and I have the privilege to say that I was the last
thing
she saw before she crossed the rainbow bridge

Raw

you can't leave me yet
please
I'm not ready

everytime I see my mom
I see you too
it's going to hurt to see her and not you

you've always been there for me as
I've been growing up

I don't remember what life
was like without you

please don't go
I need you here
with me

Sarah Cowan

It's Been One Month

it's been one month
and my heart still aches at the thought of you
the moment I felt your chest go still that day
was the moment that a part of me died with you

nothing is the same without you
life feels less colorful
more bleak as the days progress

will I ever see color again?

Unforgiving

I never thought grief would be so unforgiving
one moment you feel a sense of normal return
something you haven't felt in weeks
next moment your heart aches and you're unsure
whether you can get through the day

I never thought grief would be so gruesome
loss is like a knife stabbing into your heart
then it twists
and twists
and *twists*
until you're the one lifeless on the ground

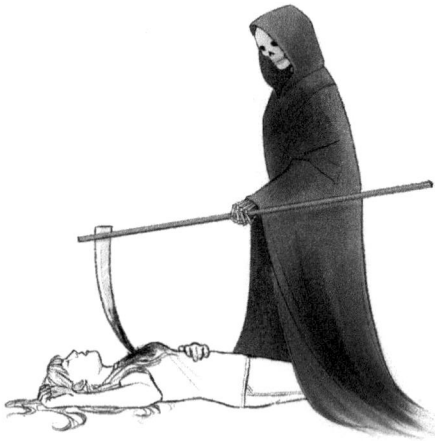

I Lost Her

my childhood died today
it wasn't until I lost her
until I realized I have nothing
from my childhood
that is worth keeping

Not A Bug

grief latches to me like a bug
that just won't go away
for my first time going through grief
I thought it would
be like the flu
over in twenty four hours

instead grief grows on you like a tree
latches to you and grows
deep roots in your heart
and it keeps nourished
by your sorrows and memories

Replacement

when I say that I miss her
I want the dead brought back to life

"just buy a new pet"
they tell me
"it'll heal a broken heart"

No.
I don't want a new pet

I want *her* fur between my fingers
hear *her* bark echo in the room
I want *her* beautiful brown eyes
staring at me, asking for a carrot
I want *my* seventeen year old baby girl
who loves belly rubs and loves sitting in the sun

I don't want a new puppy that knows nothing about
me
nor do I know anything about them
I don't want that
I want *her*
I miss my baby girl, and only my girl
a lifetime of longing for a return that'll never
happen
I don't want anybody else
don't you understand?

Paw Printed Blanket

my soul has been deflating and aching
the longer I keep your blanket with me
the blanket you took your last breath on

at first I hoped keeping this would
bring me a healing heart
but instead its bringing turmoil,
mixed emotions,
anger and lots of tears

maybe it's because we're spreading
her ashes in 2 days
is that why I keep crying?

this prized possession is shoving me
in the direction of healing and acceptance
something I have been avoiding for a while
and something I wasn't prepared to do

I haven't felt this fragile since the day I let her go
every thought feels like a weight tied onto my body
every touch of the blanket feels like
thorns against my skin

one day this won't hurt anymore
to have it in my home.

I Love You

we spread your ashes the other day
I miss you.

we scattered them back at home;
the town you were born and raised in
driving away from where your ashes lay
I felt a bit more empty than before
like I'm forgetting something
I miss you.

now when I miss you, I don't have anything to hold
onto
except your paw printed blanket
I held onto it this morning and sobbed
I miss you.

It burns when I ache for a touch
or a gentle lick on my nose
there hasn't been a day where I don't think about
you
you have yet to leave my mind
I love you.

I Miss You

I want you to know that I miss you
walking away from you was the hardest thing
I have ever had to do

I've walked away from so much in my life
but your lifeless body was the hardest
I wanted to stay by your side
keep you in my arms
but we both knew that wasn't possible

you fought long and hard
I was there every step of the way

till the last dying breath

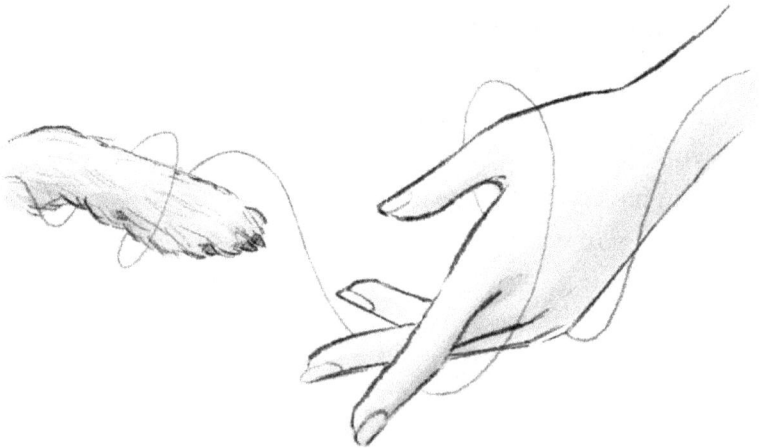

Regret

I think of all the missed time I had with you
in your last few years of life
growing older together allowed me to be with you
but I was absent in your last 5 years

I should have stayed, could have visited you more
often
there's no more would haves
because you're gone
and I can never see you again

I wasn't there for you a lot
in your last few years
it hurts knowing I grew absent when you
probably needed me the most

of course I'd visit;
but I rarely kissed you goodnight
and cuddled you in the morning
now it feels like it wasn't enough

    I'm sorry

So Hard

I wish there was an easier way to heal from grief
everyone else seems to be fine
but here I am, three months later, feeling so fragile
I rage and cry and break almost every day
because I can't accept that you are gone

every little thing sets me off
when does the healing start?
shouldn't it have started by now?

every day I wake up and feel so tired and
my soul deflates at the reminder that you're gone
and there's nothing I can do to bring you back

Aftermath

last night, I blew up
that ticking time bomb went off inside me
everything got pushed onto the floor
the clanging and banging to fill the midnight air

running to the bedroom,
he tried to talk to me but I ignored him
because I knew if I tried to say something
it would only add gas to the fire
I grabbed my coat and keys
storming out of the house
slamming the door behind me

the key shook in my hand from the built up anger
once it was nearly 1:00am
I calmed myself down
and came back home

after finally talking with him
is when I realized how fucked up I am
how poor my mental health has gotten:
feeling like or just crying all the time,
getting angry over the smallest things,
no motivation to live,
don't want to eat,
losing drive to do any of my hobbies,
refusing to accept she's gone

I'm Not Ready

I'm scared to heal
scared to let go
because if I heal from this grief
it means you disappear
the feeling you still give me
even when you're not on earth
is still a strong feeling

if I heal, you'll go away
and I don't want you to go away

maybe if I hold onto this grief for a little longer
maybe you'll stay alive in my heart

Empty

the cabinet where your items once sat
remains empty

every time it opens, I cry
three months have passed and
I can't get myself to fill your spot

"it was her cabinet", I tell my partner
when he asks me why it remains empty
"as long as I've lived here,
only her stuff was in there"

it feels wrong to fill it with items that
aren't her stuff
I just can't do it
even opening the cabinet stirs up some tears

I want that cabinet to stay empty
because it became hers
not mine

She's Dead

He always told me how it is
told me what I need to hear
not what I want to hear

"I can't accept that she's gone
if I hold onto this grief, I have this thought
that it'll keep her alive."
I cried to him last night

"you can't bring her back to life
holding onto your grief won't keep her alive
she's dead."

those two very last words cut me so deep
I felt like I was going to bleed out
on that couch I sat on
the rivers rush from my eyes
thinking on this harsh reality I've been avoiding
for now four months
a reality I'm not ready to come to terms with

it's true; she is dead
everything he said is right
I just can't get myself to accept it yet
I know if I accept her passing, I can begin to heal
I'm aware of this necessary step in my journey

but it's like I'm standing on the edge of the deepest
cliff
staring into the pit of an empty void
I can't jump
I can't heal
I feel stuck on this edge
and can't find the courage to
fall into this healing
that I know will be healthier for me
than this internal pit of despair

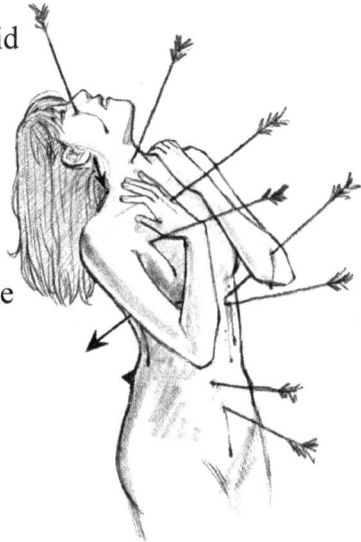

Grief with Grace

you don't know grief until you do

once Grim grazes you for the first time
his plague never leaves you
the dark cloud looming above your head
constantly stays, no matter how many times
you try to swat it all away

part of me wishes I could go back
to the old me who didn't know what grief is

because now I need to
carry this grief with grace
for the rest of my life

You Were Here

it hurts to remember that one year ago
you were here

and now you're not

Not The Same

the first year after their passing
is the absolute worst

it's the first time out of many
they will miss every holiday:
every christmas, every new years,
every birthday–especially their own
now you'll be left blowing out
their candles in their absence

the first 365 days without them stings the most
it's not the same without them
they occupy a spot in your heart always
but that's the only place of yours that they'll fit

First Time

you have been my first for many things:
my first true love
and now my first true grieving

I never wanted you to leave me
holding onto you
I never wanted to envision a world without you

now that is my new reality
I'll never see you again
even on the days my soul breaks from missing you

Me VS The World

I truly hated the world when you left
why did heaven need you more than me?

I begged the universe for an explanation
crying at the fact that I now will go to sleep
and wake up the next morning
knowing that this isn't a dream

no matter how much I want to see you live
I'll forever fight with the world
trying to see you again

Sarah Cowan

Time Passes

months after you were gone
I thought the bug was over
that I've finally healed

I was so wrong

I nearly fooled myself with
thinking I was okay again

the girl staring back at me
in the mirror looked otherwise
sunken eyes,
deflated posture,
aching soul

if grief embodied a person
I would've been it

Picture Imperfect

pictures look familiar, but yet feel unusual
all those memories don't look the same
when they're gone
a moment of bliss turns into an empty void
realizing you'll never get a photo with them again

I look at every photo differently now
before I used to see them as memories
now they're images I long to relive
over and over again

Grief

people say that grief is love but with
no place to go

through learning about grief
I find myself sprinkling this love in desperate places

hugging your blanket when I need
to feel closer to you

looking at pictures and videos when I want
to remember what life was like with you

staying glued to my computer to write
bleeding out these poems to keep you alive

when I can't accept you're gone and I
still feel all of this love that's supposed to go to you
I try and find ways to keep you alive
when I can only now long for your impossible
resurrection

Shocked

"I feel like out of everyone in the family,
I've been handling this grief the worst."
I said, but they seemed shocked
"Oh really?" they said with astounded
yet sympathetic eyes

why are you shocked?
five months later and I'm still crying
at the thought of her
and let me guess
you moved on five months ago?

why are you shocked?
should I have moved on faster?
am I the broken one who can't let her go?
what's wrong with me?

why are you shocked?
how else should I have reacted?
why don't you tell me how I can
just stop feeling like this

Depression

I wake up dragging my feet
praying today will be better

work is a distraction and I'm grateful for it
when I'm at home
the mask comes off.
I get cemented to my couch and I'm stuck
I can't live like everyone else

I can't get myself to cook
I can't get myself to eat a proper meal
I can't get myself to shower as often as I used to
I can't get myself to bring back old hobbies

"I just wanted to see what's wrong
you haven't done any hobbies lately"
he said to me the other night
sitting across from him lifelessly
I didn't know what to say

I don't know what's happening in my head
I don't know when it'll get better
I don't know if I'll love life again

Better Off Dead

I am beyond depressed
I suffer instead of living through my days
would I be better off dead?
this grieving pain is near unbearable
there is no joy sparked in my life anymore
it's all been sucked away from me

every day and night I sit on my couch and rot
doom scrolling and starving myself because
I don't have the motivation to even
get something to eat
none of my hobbies give me joy anymore

so I've stopped them.

why do I have emotions?
can't I just go back to feeling numb?
suppressing everything to feel nothing
mourning has never left my mind
and it clings to my aching soul

now I get so angry
but for what reason?
every tiny thing makes me want to scream
my heart aches so much
it travels and stings my body

I feel paralyzed at the thought of you
I feel unwell at the thought of you
I feel like maybe I'd be better off dead too
that way I can't feel anything anymore

RESILIENCE

Emotionally Unstable

life is tough but darling you are tougher

loss makes everyone emotionally unstable
so don't feel alone

maybe you'll burn your wedding dress
in the dead of winter
or cry so much as you're driving
that you can't see the road
loss makes you so unbelievably fragile
the smallest inconvenience will feel
like the end of the world
this feeling isn't the end
there is still hope, and lots of it

hope starts with one simple action:
asking for help
whether it's an ear to listen to or
someone to keep an eye on you
there is always someone who would
want to listen to you
rather than attending your funeral
next time you feel emotionally unstable
know that this is not the end

Stinging Silver

that necklace you gave me back then
I threw it away

there came a point in my life where
I couldn't stand it sitting on my nightstand
it haunted me every time I stepped in my bedroom

I knew that one piece of jewelry
was the last piece of you that I had
it was the only thing left I could grasp onto

and for so long, I held onto it
refusing to let go

in order for me to move on,
I had to throw it away
for me to let you go,
I had to let the necklace go

it pained me watching the silver pendent
slip through my fingertips
but I knew that I had to

I could never tell you that
but now you know

Cut Off

nothing compares to grieving someone
who is still alive
losing touch with someone who once
filled your cup with happiness
so much so that the cup often
was seen overflowing

even when you know it might
be best for your
wellbeing to let someone go
they still sit in your heart
occupying a small space that
will always be theirs

even if it's not what you want
you know deep down that it is
what you need

Let Them

let them hate you
let them loathe your existence
it is not your responsibility to ensure that
everyone loves you

love yourself for who you are
the good
the bad
and the ugly

with seven billion people on earth
someone is bound to hate you
and there is nothing you can do about it

First

be the first to raise your hand
the first to speak your mind
the first to make a difference

many stay hushed in fears
of causing too much chaos

but let the world hear your call
standing on the sidelines
will only get you so far

Run Away

many run from discomfort

don't

don't let fear stop you from jumping
into the deep end
from kissing that boy you know loves you
or from waiting for "the right time"

your right time is *now*
do not run away from things that
could give you a thrill
or a lifelong memory

Unrequited Love

like the sun, their love was
far away yet always present

she could feel her sunshine
being ripped from her
her love was never in her reach
but she felt the heat
only when he was willing
to come around

Not Like She Used To

once upon a time
a girl fell in love with a boy
they shared all kinds of joyous memories

eventually they fell out of love
time separated them and
they were no longer compatible

as time went by
she still cared for him
but not like she used to

it's a different kind of care
it's hard to stop loving someone completely
when they once meant everything to you

a soft spot kept in her heart
a "I hope they're doing okay"
or "I wonder what they're doing nowadays"

she still cares for him, but not like she used to

Freshest Air

how beautiful it is to know
that realizing you deserve better
can be the biggest breath of
the freshest air you could ever breathe

Too Much

when life feels too much
the air feels too heavy to breathe
I will look for peace within
leaning to close friends and family

I will listen to the songs orchestrated by the birds
or smell the fresh scent of rain
for the reassurance from the world
telling me that peace will lift
this feeling of everything being too much

Strength

you broke me
I handed you my heart
in hopes you won't break it

but you did

you let go of my heart
letting it shatter on the floor
nearly killing me

because of you
I now know my strength

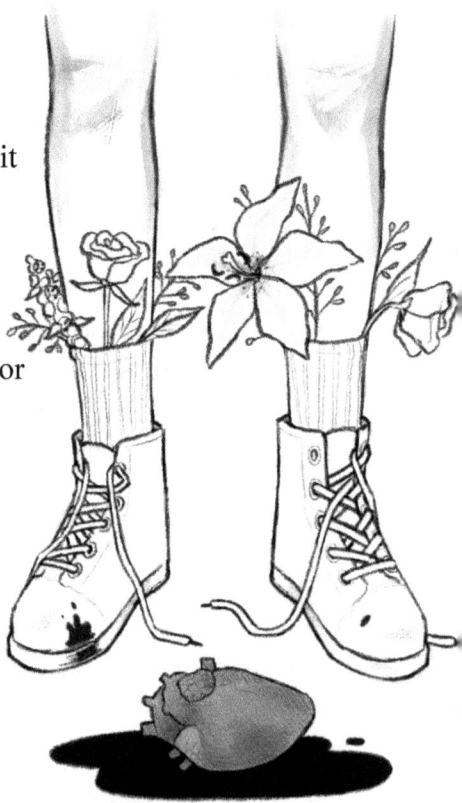

Castle

I used to look at him as my other half
the foundation to my castle
the sun to my blue sky
without him
there is no me

when my castle started to crumble
is when I realize he is not the foundation
I have built my own castle
brick by brick
he is simply an addition to the
beauty that surrounds me
a flower sitting outside

Still Standing

pushing me down more and more
making me wonder if there really is good
in this world
negative on negative
it keeps getting worse

but I keep standing up
after every bullet pounding into my chest
I manage to still stay on my feet

bad things happen
but it's all about not letting it take you down

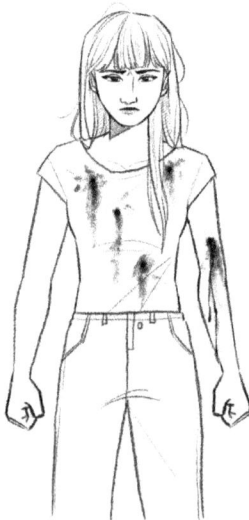

Back Then

I didn't think everything
was going to be okay
going through the worst of my life
I thought there was no ending
no light at the end of the tunnel

back then, I didn't want to accept that
this too shall pass
that clouds do part
negative emotions are temporary

as years has passed
I see it has gotten better

The Rug

you ripped the rug out
from under my mind
I felt destined to fall
like I have many times
I may have stumbled
but I tried to catch myself

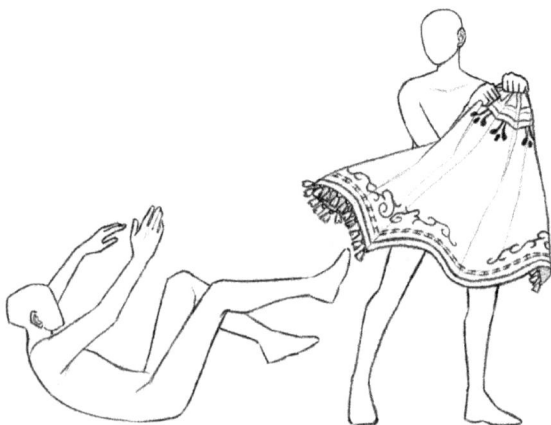

It's Not Your Fault

one thing I've learned in my years of living is this:

never *ever* put your happiness in someone else's
hands

they will drop it
every time
people can be unreliable
but keeping your happiness in your own hands
ensure that you won't break

when things go astray, many tend to blame
themselves
but honey, don't you ever say it's your fault
your life is destined for greatness
if something didn't go your way
it must've just been a learning lesson
don't blame yourself because if it was meant to
happen
it will happen.

Irreplaceable

every dog I've walked past since the day
I sent you across the rainbow bridge
revolts me
I can't get another dog

never

though she is irreplaceable
every dog I see isn't *my* dog
it's just *a* dog

my best friend is waiting for me
on the other side of that bridge

Tattoo

tattoo ink bleeds your love
your little paw print is now
permanently etched on my arm
right near my heart

now whenever I miss you
all I need to do is look down
and know that you are now walking with me
through my track of life

just like I have for you

Habit

I find myself looking where you once laid
hoping I'll see you resting your head
in a peaceful slumber
chest raising and lowering in a noiseless rhythm

instead I look there and find the empty floor
you're not there
your bed is gone and toys are put away
the floor is bare without you living here
I didn't realize what a habit I needed to break
until you left me

a new habit of silence
of needing to stop looking where you once laid
or knowing I don't need to keep an eye
on your food bowl
making sure you're always cared for

it's all a new habit
one that might be hard to break
but not impossible

just a new habit to get used to

Ready

I used to tell myself I wasn't ready
that healing wasn't even an option
because if I healed you would disappear

it took me a while to realize that you *are* here
with me
right now
every day
for the rest of my life
and that you will never leave my side

I have come to terms that you are no longer
that seeing you isn't in my house of cards anymore
doesn't mean I can't feel you
that you protect me even if I can't see you
I feel your presence

and I think I'm finally ready to heal

Enduring Love

though her body is no longer
since she's left I've learned that
my love for her has never felt stronger

I'm grateful that as we both got older
I knew I had to take every picture of her that I could
knowing one day it'll be the only time
that I could hold her

hearing your bark on a video brings back the
reminder
of how our enduring love lives on
even though I'm no longer beside her

Sarah Cowan

It Doesn't Hurt Like It Did

today I kept looking at your pictures
reliving videos and keeping you alive
any way that I could

and for the first time in so long, I smiled
a grin grew upon my face reliving
all those happy memories I wish
I could go back and relive
for once I didn't cry

my heart throbbed but didn't ache
I miss her but I remember her with happy memories
her final moments slowly faded

I smiled just a bit wider
knowing that I'm healing
just like she would've hoped for me

Onward

it's not about moving on from it
it's about moving forward

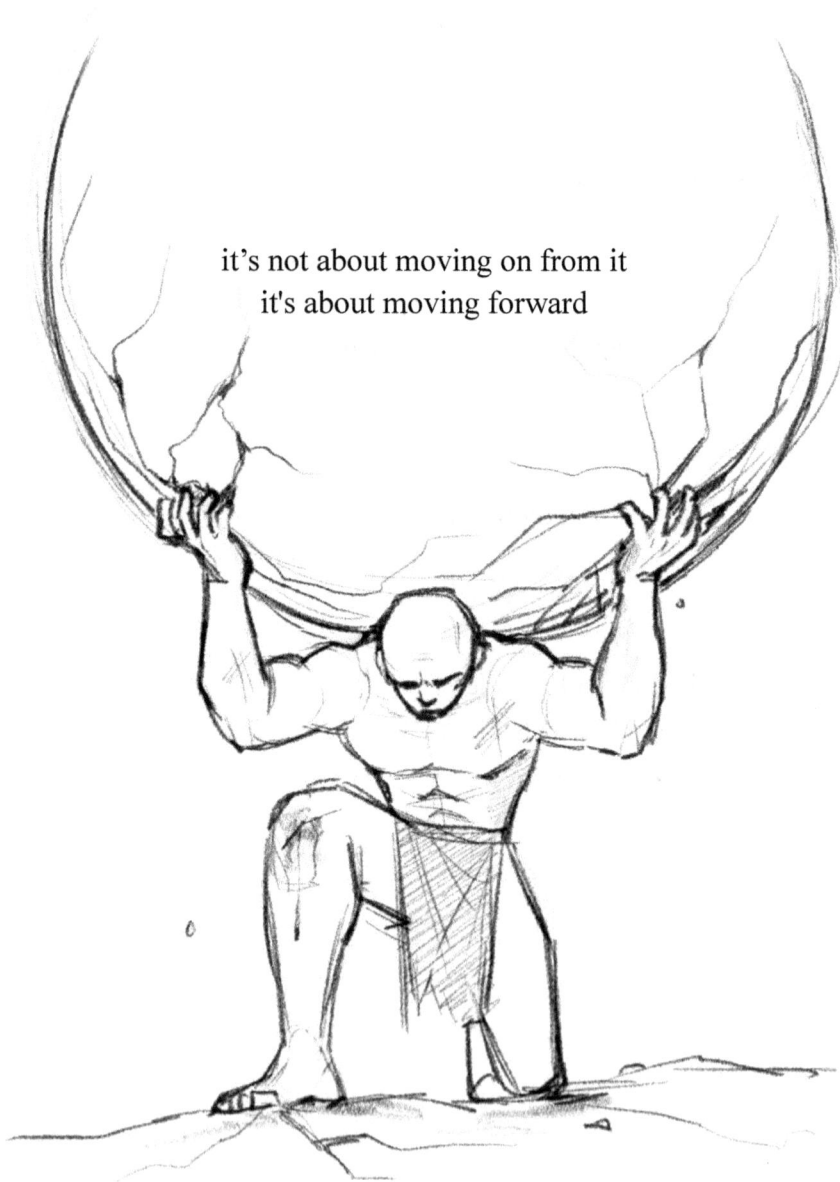

Death

in the sorrows of death
is the proof of love

that bonds exist beyond what our reality sees
and past the matter and energy
that makes our world real

See You Later

I stroked your fur one last time
feeling your grays and browns between my
fingertips
my heart dazed and eyes dry
"I'll see you later" I kissed your head softly

I hate goodbyes
so I say "see you later"
makes the ending less harsh
and that is exactly what I told you
I will see you later
maybe not soon. But one day
one day I'll see you again
with tears flowing down my face
we will reunite once again

I saw the life leave your body
your chest that never inhaled again
placing my hand upon it
I hoped to feel your heartbeat
one more time

leaving you behind I knew that
this will be the greatest pain that I will carry

Petals Not Thorns

your blanket used to hurt
to look at or to touch
like thorns on a rose
it used to hurt me

now I'm not afraid to touch the
paw printed blanket
now I touch it as I walk past to tell you that I love
you
and get just a little bit closer to you

having your last breath on this blanket
doesn't plague my thoughts anymore

this soft blanket brings comfort to my fingertips
not cutting thorns like it once did

Echoes Of Your Presence

I went to visit the river alone today
last time I stood here was when my family and I
scattered your ashes
hiding myself in between the towering grass
I sat down in front of the water

"I miss you." I whispered into the air
hoping that you'd hear me
"I wish healing from you was easier."

the longer I sat, the more peaceful it became
no tears, no heaviness
not even a single depressing thought I believed
this place would provoke
I would just stare at the scenery
absorbing the quietness you bring me

I feel you
by my side, sitting with me by the water
it's like you were making the wind
wrap me in their arms
telling me that you are right beside me
on the river bank

Sarah Cowan

Do You See Me?

when I stare longingly into those
orange and purple skies
or maybe the starry night
are you looking down at me too?

95

Echoes Of Paws

I can still hear your collar tags ting together
as you would walk across the floor
I can still hear your nails, ticking on the ground
as you walk around
I can still hear your bark
even though you were often very quiet
I can still hear you moving your food bowl around
as you were making a mess doing so

I'll never forget every little sound
you brought to my life
another sensation of you still lingering in my life
you're never away from me

you're always here with me
just in a different form

Whispers Of The Heart

she is the wind wrapping around my body
the bird sitting on my balcony railing
or orange and red skies shining
after a long and tiring day

her spirit is always with me
like a quiet whisper or a guiding star

Healing In Silence

in your absence, I eventually began to heal
accepting what was true
in her silence, I began to reflect on our lives
and how we grew up together
every hug, every thrown toy
every holiday we spent together

all this quiet reflection made me realize that
our bond was so much deeper than I even realized
I ache and hurt because I've never lost something
so close to my heart before

Poem and the Poet

now you are reborn to be a poem
and I chose to be your poet

Garden of Memories

when we first brought you home
we planted our first seed
as we loved and cared for you over seventeen years
thousands of seeds were planted and cared for
all flowering into a bountiful and glorious garden

every blooming seed that we once buried in the soil
is a cherished memory
for me, for her or for our family

once she left the garden and we no longer had any
seeds
I planted our first weed
the plaguing thought of watching
you take your last breath
the weed spread and spread
infecting the rest of the garden of memories
at first, I nearly let it all die

Sarah Cowan

I finally chose to pick the weed from my garden
and set it off to the side
not away permanently, just out of the garden
this weed is ruining the loving seeds that we've
already
planted, loved and cared for
that hurtful weed needed to go

it needed to go so we can all remind ourselves that
we must care for the garden
and admire the beautiful flowers that have
grown from the little seeds we planted

we need to cherish the garden of memories
even when there are no more seeds to plant

Numb

it's hard to describe what nothing feels like
it feels like nothing and everything at once
tears knock on those flood gates
but your head sucks up all the tears like a sponge

it's feeling like you're going crazy
from losing feeling in your heart
is it normal to not cry?
normal to feel nothing when
everyone else around you
is feeling everything?

losing feeling in my heart is apart of
the mourning journey

one day, I will feel again

Flashback

every so often I get flashbacks
of when she left me

I feel like I get teleported back to that day
feeling the sense of hopelessness and loss
of where I'll find joy without her
the reminder of the details in her fur
struggling to walk out the clinic doors
and leave her behind

sometimes I get lost thinking that every holiday is
going through it for the first time without her

sometimes I feel like all my healing has gone
all because a single memory decided to make a
return

Talk To Me

I always think about you
how are you doing?
do you miss being here on earth?
but you were hurting in your last months
do you miss your family that you left behind?
but not the pain life gave you?
I have so many questions for you
I wish you could answer even one of them

I miss you
but I don't miss seeing you in pain anymore

Sarah Cowan

New Year

as the new year breaks a new dawn
I try not to let it sting my thoughts that
she will stay in last year
unable to follow me into the new year

it burns knowing that I keep living on
and you will stay behind
a new calendar year is the hard reminder
that life does not stop for anyone
and that time does continue on

into a new year, I will try to carry you with me
even though all I want is for you to be here
in the physical world

Paw Prints From Heaven

the brisk winter air brought me back to the river
where we scattered your ashes in the summer
something was pulling me to come back to see you
or, quite likely, someone was pulling me back

as I trudge through the shin-high snow
going where we all stood many months ago
I couldn't help but notice there was animal prints
that steered me off the sidewalk
and exactly to where I was hoping to stand
in the same place we scattered your ashes

are those dog paw prints?
maybe paw prints from heaven?
there's not even a human print nearby
could easily be a deer, maybe a roaming dog
but I like to think that these are her footprints
letting me know that she is with me
by the riverfront once more

Sarah Cowan

SELF DISCOVERY

Keep Shining

admit it

you know you have a blissful soul
never listen to someone if they
attempt to dull your shine
let your light shine bright
brighter than the sun above us

don't hide something you were born with
whether it be a smile, a curve, or a stretch mark

a blank canvas is only beautiful
when it is covered in art

have you ever seen someone
praise a blank canvas?

Overflowing Cup

you can't run a car when there's no gas

many keep giving to people when
their cup to give is bone dry
they scavenge for pieces to offer
even when there's nothing else to give

fill your personal fulfillment cup first
fill it so full that the fullness flows off the sides
focusing on yourself will make you happier
but then it will also make you less drained when
you
are needing to give to others
when you find self fulfillment
giving to others becomes that much easier

Science

before I could really grow up
I needed to look within
relearning everything about myself
about why I am the way I am

why I cower in every argument
why I was too desperate to find love back then
why I fear everything will go wrong at any point

looking within to find all the answers
was not an easy journey
for every action, there is always a reaction

it was a science to learn who I am
it is a lifelong progress that will never end

Sensitive Souls

what a shame it is that not everyone
can feel as deeply as you do

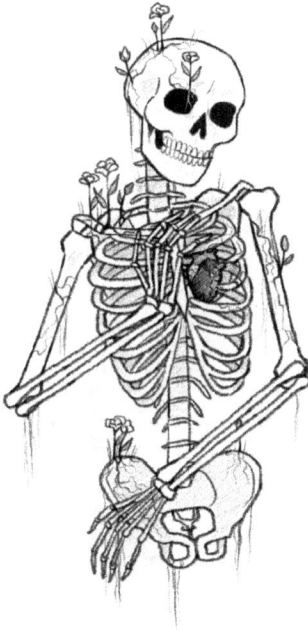

Thousand Ways

so many poems are written about you
the words ooze your memories
and my sorrow

reliving the hurt and reliving the pain
no matter how many times I write it
or how many different ways I'll say it
it'll all boil down to the same thing
over and over again:

I loved you and you left me

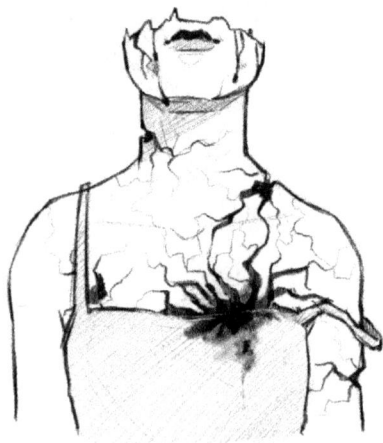

Sarah Cowan

Free

many years ago
this child you see
was once a young girl
scared and oblivious to her future

unaware of the change
the accomplishments
and the pain
of what's to come

but here she stands
freer than she ever has been
growing and evolving every day
creating her masterpiece

day by day
she lets the wind soar
beneath her wings
letting the wind guide
her to where she needs to be

Naked

I never knew how naked I have become
until I began to share all of my dreams
to you, for your enjoyment

a goal that makes me who I am
something I strive to become
I realize I shed all layers of my mask
to share with you who I really want to be in life

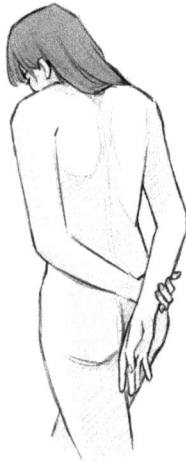

Used To Be

I miss who I used to be
youthful
joyous
and innocent

but the broken adult that I am
still deserves love too

Was It Me?

all along I thought you were
the villain in our narrative
the one who left
the one who forced me to heal without closure
the one who hurt me

then one day, it struck me:
was I the problem all along?

back then, I didn't fully realize that
I gave you an ultimatum:
talk to me
or nothing at all
and that made you push me away completely
I clung desperately to you
when all you needed was space

I invaded that

I see that now
now I'm left with the weight of my mistake
living with the regret
that I was the one who pushed you away—

not the other way around

What's Worse?

healing doesn't come easy
it is gruesome
it is bitter
feeling like an endless cycle of
ease and pain

but what's worse?
constant heartache
or learning to heal that
aching heart of yours?

I Am. . .

I am waves crashing upon the sandy shore
bright lit moon on a dark night
an eagle flying high above the trees

I am a shattered wine glass
a child's laughter as they run through the grass
lady justice representing good and fairness
to those around her

I am a metaphor of all new and broken

I am poetry

Ode to Self

you are me and I am you
we look the same, but I look more tired
older, maybe wiser
but all the pain that lives on
has elapsed

why does she feel so exhausted?
so hurt?
so drained?

why can't her heart heal?
ease the pain of all the hurt?

she wonders why
and the thought
merely haunts her
every
single
day

but then she realizes
that she doesn't

she doesn't have to hurt like this

Years

it took me years to finally come to terms
that you do not benefit me no more
that final string that tied our hearts together
needed to be cut

using my best scissors, I cut that final tie
though I hoped you would be there for me
all you did was teach me a lesson

and I learned everything I needed to
I learned what I expect in a partner
learned that I don't need to beg
for someone to love me

for years, I longed for your return
after so many years
I had lost count,
that's when I knew it was time
time to let you go
time to cut that string

I need to move on
just like you have years ago

Healing

that one conversation we had,
gave me more answers than I
have ever searched for

I learned you never cheated like I thought
and you genuinely regret what you did to me
I learned that you can admit your flaws to me
and you apologized for hurting me back then
I learned I meant more to you than I felt
and you told me you're grateful to have me forgive
you

all along I thought you never cared for me
and here we are, nearly eight years later
having a conversation like adults and giving me the
healing that I dreamed of
for so long

thank you

Soul Garden

she planted all the seeds in her soul garden
as her flowers grew, people plucked the ones
they wanted
even if they were the most beautiful ones that grew
if they were feeling really spiteful
they would stomp on her garden
crushing her down till everything has died

starting all over again
she planted all the seeds in her soul garden
as her flowers grew, she fed all her flowers
the proper food to make them strong and tall
people no longer came to keep her buds
she realized she valued her garden
only giving her flowers
to those who deserve it
fighting those who try to pull her down
and steal the best parts of her

Hurt Me

hurt the artist of my life, I dare you
life has already beaten you to it
it wasn't me who caused this fire
I am just the one who tries to put it out

hurt me because I will create
something great from it
from all the ashes, sobs and to laying lifeless on my
bed
feeling nothing makes me feel something

craving to ooze the pain onto paper
I will take this hurt and do something
most can't do

hurt me and you will see
the greatest masterpiece from what you've done

Magnetic Pull

years has passed from when we
once loved each other
and there you are
standing before me
both of us frozen
unable to move

as we are magnets in this world
the universe pulled us back together
until we're standing in front of each other
questioning who is supposed to speak first

it's been six years since you broke my heart
or have even talked to me
but here you stand
"I've missed you." he softly blurted
those three words echoed in my ears
making my heart trip on itself

but then
I woke up

Forget

I often forget what it is like
to be gentle with myself

to look in the mirror
at every scar and curve
and love what I see

speak to myself with
kind words and
look at myself
with loving eyes

Parallel Universe

in a different world
we never said hi to each other
you walked right past me that day
while you were heading to class
we never texted nor fell in love

in a parallel universe
we never knew what it would be
like to fall in love together
or to fall apart even worse

Rainbow

all my life I was taught to be the rainbow
in everyone's life
please people
make them happy

as I got older I realized that I need to be the
rainbow for myself
not for everyone who knows me

cherish my love for myself
set boundaries
and make myself the priority

I learned that I need to
stop being a rainbow to the people
who are blind to see it

For The People

her words echoed in my mind
sending them on repeat over and over again:

Don't people please your way out of what you want

until that very moment, I never took into
consideration as to what I want in life
my life
my ambitions
my happiness

this life I live always has
revolved around everyone else
very rarely do I ever take into consideration
what I want or what makes me happy
and what I do has always been for the people

it has only been right here, right now
that the blinds have opened and the
knowledge of sunlight has beamed down upon me
only now have I finally realized that
I am the people
I am the person I need to prioritize

I am living for myself, not for the people anymore

Gift of Time

pain brings gifts that many struggle to see
the loss of our beloved dog gave
her a gift

the gift of time

the ability to visit her friends as late as she wants
to book in that dentist appointment
she's put off for months, maybe even years
to sleep in, without the rush of going for a walk

the gift of time is a glorious gift
it's hard to see it as an offering at first
but it is a gift to cherish

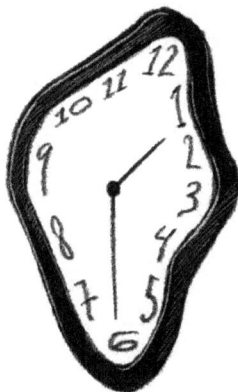

Final Walk

I can recall your final walk well
I held your worn blue leash as you slowly led the
way.
being the leader on a route you're all too familiar
with

we were all aware this will be the last time
that we all walk these sidewalks with you

a heaviness filled the air and I don't even think
you knew why we were so upset
I began to silently cry as cars roared past
breaking little by little
trying to absorb this moment as
much as my broken heart can

I write this to remember that
I have yet to walk on that sidewalk again

I'm Sorry

death made me realize the
importance of time

though you lived for seventeen years
I was with you for eleven years

moving out into my own place
I thought I'd love independence
but I realized too late that me moving out
caused distance between us

I missed out on your last six years
and I now live in agony
knowing I could have
stayed to love you better
love you more

Dream

you visited me in a dream again
you looked different
your furry face was smiling at me
tail wagging happily

I felt your presence
it was *you*
I know it truly was your spirit
it had to be

it's like you were telling me
"I'm okay, look how happy I am
look how pain free I am
I'm showing you how much better I am"

Life After Death

death taught me that there truly is life after death
the sun will shine again
you will laugh till you cry
you will think about them
and not want to crack into an ocean of tears

when death brought my world to a halt
I truly thought it was over
I didn't think I'd be able to find any joy
in anyone or anything

but here I am
able to look back on our memories
and it doesn't break me in so many pieces

the cracks in my heart are still there
but they're more together than long ago
time helped heal the wound
that I thought would take me out

Rebrand

when you left this world
I was forced to refind myself
reconstructing my beliefs and values
and what makes me tick

death sucks
but what's worse is the repercussion
of trying to heal on your own
I lost myself while
she lost her purpose

I learned I turn to creative outlets to heal
my heart pouring out onto these pages
each line has become a stitch
mending me back together

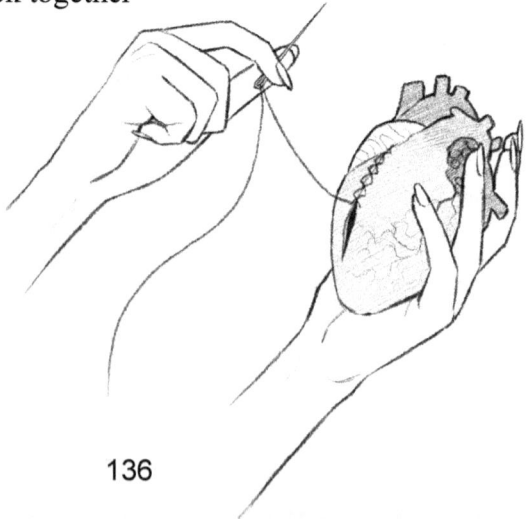

Lesson

going through grief for the first time as an adult
gave me an opportunity to really turn within
and see how I grieve the loss of someone I love

I went numb
I couldn't feel anything for a month
but when I did finally feel genuine grief
for the first time
it was like I suddenly was drowning above water

losing my breath and my life
from something I can't control

everyday I suffered
for weeks
for months
until one day, I didn't want to cry
where I looked at your picture and longed for a
touch
but I knew that you're beside me always

you were a hard lesson to learn
but you should see the growth it gave me

2:34pm

the moment you passed, I checked the time
my watch illuminated reading "2:34pm"
as a believer in angel numbers
that was no coincidence she passed at that exact
time
and that I looked at my watch
at
that
exact
time

2:34 means I was progressing and moving
forward in my path
that tough times are soon behind me
how convenient, huh?

It took me a long time to see the vision
that was made for me
I hurt for so long before I could finally breathe
again
but seeing that time on the clock when I did
I see it gave me the reassurance
before I knew what it was;
that the worst is over
and all I needed to do was focus on healing

Bad Days

clocks go round and round
making me dizzy
time passes and I feel a pit of ache

today is a bad day
yesterday was a good day though
but today I long for her just a bit more

despite being pulled down by the weight of her
not here anymore
I know that I don't want her back

I don't want the girl who was hurting
and not living life freely anymore

living yet another bad day
I know that she is having all kinds of good days
up in heaven as she looks down upon me

Slow and Steady

hard to think six months has already flown past
it feels like I just lost you forever ago
her boundless love that we can never outlast
being with her felt like my sunshine yellow

losing her made me heal in crazy ways
jumping off the deep end, drowning in the shower
"But you're doing so well," they praised
little do they know, I just heal slower

everyone has healed at different paces
didn't the turtle win all those races?

X marks the Spot

grief is a journey to an unknown place
a map stained with tears and remembrance
each step guiding me to who I am
fueled by the love that still remains

N

Dead End

in the so-called end, I found a beginning
after the fire burned all of what was left
a little sprout came through the ashes

in my mourning, I was remade
rebuilt from burnt out embers
loss proved there was never
a dead end

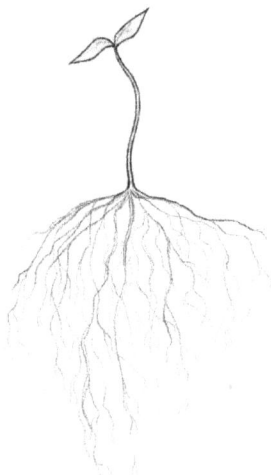

I See Now

lifting the veil of grief, I began to dig within
bringing forward different pieces to the light
even letting the shadows be seen
as I was stripped from everything that I once knew
I stood there bare and alone
and only then, was I finally able to see
see the rawness of death and mourning

Soul Dog

six months ago I still remember how
I stayed close to her side
one hand on her chest, ensuring I feel that last
exhale
the other hand, giving reassuring pets

I am convinced that day, when air emptied from
her lungs one last time
her soul traveled up through my hand
and she nestled into my heart

for the past six months
I feel her presence around me
always feeling like I'm not alone
always having a youthful dog spirit hovering
around me in every point of my life

I lost my soul dog six months ago
but our bond goes beyond the physical
I've never felt more connected to her than after
she left me

a soul dog's bond never goes unmatched

Gone

as time has passed me by
I've learned that the saddest word
in the English language
has become burned in my heart;

gone

when something or someone is gone
a return is now only a dream
feeling the warmth of their body
is now impossible
every night you get met with the sorrows
of their absence

something you can never get back
all because they're gone

Juxtaposition

with confidence, I can say that
2024 has been both the best
and the worst year of my life so far
I have seen myself at my highest of highs
yet comforted myself at my lowest of lows

going to three concerts and smiling so wide
my face hurts
experience living with my partner
for the first time
being so happy that tears glide down my cheeks
traveling to new places, experiencing new things
the feeling of wanting to live in this moment forever

to watch someone I love take their last breath
spiraling for months, feeling that maybe
I should be dead too
watching everything fall into place
for everyone else
while I can only fall apart

but as a new year lurks my way
I can only be grateful for the strength
and growth this year alone has given me

Spinning Circles

I feel that grief is never linear.
one day I am fine, probably in the acceptance phase
tomorrow I'm in my depression
and cry at the thought of wanting to hug her again
the day after I'm strong and feel like
nothing is wrong
but by the end of the week, I feel
as if I'm back in denial

my head is spinning faster than I can comprehend
it's like I've become completely unpredictable
I jump from each phase without any preparation

healing is not linear
but as time passes, it will get easier

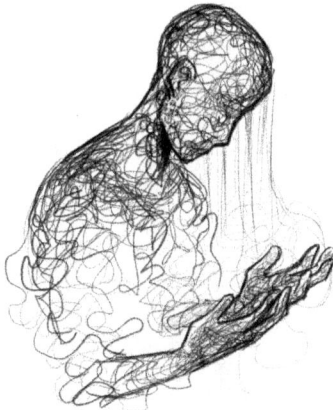

May 11th

I will think of you every May
snow is melting and the seasons are changing
every May is the time of year where winter finally
left
but it's when you left too

as the seasons changed to something new
I have learned to adapt with the seasons
still missing you the same
I just learned to grieve easier

Together Again

when we brought you home for the first time
we got you as a family
my parents loved you deeply from the start
as my sister and I cuddled you
and the three of us played in the backyard

years went by and we all grew up and grew older
parents got divorced
older sister moved out
then I later moved out on my own too
until my mother was your sole caretaker

when it came for us to put you down
all four of us went back together as a family
for you

it warmed my heart knowing we brought
you home as a family many years ago
and now we are sending you away
still as a family

as we were together again that day
it was the least we could do for you

Love & Loss

experiencing grief in your twenties
doesn't feel right
too young to feel that touch of death
attempting to live normally
and still have all those other life experiences
ahead of you

how do I continue life without you?

trying to live freely and make new memories
feel like it's all a plan
destined to fail

how can I accept this young that I could
grieve this loss longer than I've known them?
remembering grief every time you see any
loved one age one year at a time

learning grief in your twenties hurts
but I know one of these days, I will find myself
back into your presence once again
while the people I love are back home only
at the beginning of their journey
of love and loss

Sarah Cowan

STARTING ANEW

Invisible String

I never met you yet
but we grew up in the same small town

I never met you yet
but we had common friends but never met each
other

I never met you yet
but I attended your high school graduation
without knowing you were there

I never met you yet
but we went to all the same schools
and had the same teachers

Sarah Cowan

the universe kept us apart yet so close for so long
saying, "they're not ready for you yet
I'll pull you two together when it's time"

but that special time finally came around
we met at our friends' wedding
you are standing as a groomsmen
and me as a bridesmaid

the invisible string pulled us tight
love must've been in the air because
it was love at first sight

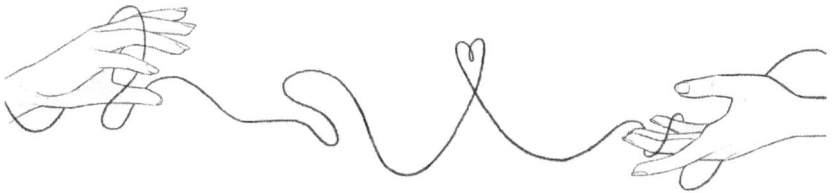

Us

if I was to tell someone about what a soulmate is
like
I'd tell them about us

I'd tell them about the butterflies
I got when I heard you unlock my front door
after I haven't seen you in weeks
about the loving way you'd stare into my eyes
how you'd open the door for me, letting me go first
you noticing the smallest mood shift
then immediately trying to spark joy for me
and it worked every damn time

I would tell them about how you would
lift me up during my darkest days
whether it's by kissing me in my ticklish spots
encouraging me or simply listening
or maybe even humoring me by doing
something I want to do
even if you don't like it

I would tell them that a soulmate loves you
at all points in your life
they would call you absolutely beautiful
even if you're fully clothed
with the messiest hair

I would share everything that you have been for me

Giving

"my partner posted me on social media"
"look at the flowers I got from them"

well he brought my spark back
he helped heal a heart he didn't break
making me laugh until I cry
or wiping away any tears of sadness

he makes me feel safe in every situation
he read me like a book and
falls in love with the fine print
rereading every page

he is the reason I've changed
calling me beautiful every single day
till I learned to listen to him and love myself too

he may not shower me in gifts
but he consistently showers me
in love and support
something that outweighs all gifts

We Just Fit

like a missing puzzle piece, you have just fit
into my life, in my heart, and in my soul
I know you can't always see me, but I will always
admire you lovingly, even when you're not looking

I've never felt such a strong connection
with another human before
you get me
you love me effortlessly

what more can I ever ask for?

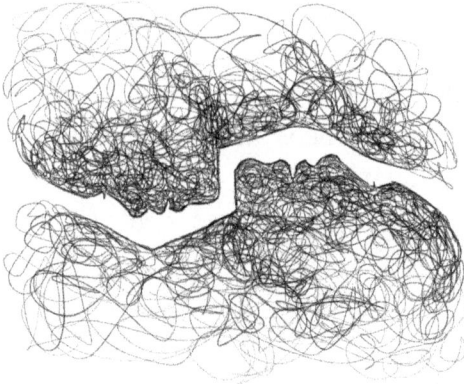

Calm

I find peace in you

when storm clouds roll above my head
you are the one that brings me calm
what is it that makes me feel peaceful?
seeing the rays of orange and red on a summer
night?
hearing the salty waves crash upon a sandy shore?
blasting your loud music with the car windows
down?
yes, I feel peaceful in all of that

you are all of that
when I talk to you, my anger dissolves
and my sadness washes away
silence and peace graces my
presence when you're around
not a thought stirs in my mind

coming into my life with hurricanes of chaos
I now know that chaos serves me no purpose
that is ruining my peace
within myself and around me

Insert Their Name Here

they make love feel real
it's like the Saturday sun gleaming through the
window
with birds orchestrating a song made just for you
driving down the road with the windows down
music louder than the wind soaring past

they know you better than you know yourself
reading and rereading your pages
highlighting their favorite part

someone is running through your mind
as your eyes read about your forever

I have never once said their name
but you know we're all thinking of that
special someone

Imagine

I romanticize on the idea of us
moving into our new home together
sharing the same door key
and cooking for the two of us
I imagine what it'd be like when
we make a house our home

I romanticize on the idea of us
finally being pronounced husband and wife
sharing the same last name
and standing in front of our closest
friends and family, reading off our
vows we spent weeks writing
I imagine what it'd be like when
we're bound by a ring and our eternal love

I romanticize on the idea of us
traveling the world
sharing the same adventure
and experiencing new cultures
I imagine what it'd be like when
we book all these trips in our lifetime

Sarah Cowan

I romanticize on the idea of us
going gray and getting wrinkles together
sharing the same smile lines from
laughing so much in our youth
going out to local cafes for our daily cup of coffee

I imagine what it'd be like when
all of these beautiful years has passed
I'll get to look back and see that
you were there for me, every step of the way

As One

he is the sun
always there, even behind the clouds
feeling steady warmth just from his presence
there has never been a hotter star
that burns in his heart

she is the moon
ever changing yet everlasting
awake while others dream
she has many sides to her, a part is always hidden
her beauty glows in the darkest of times

the sun and moon are inseparable
her moon glistens from his light
he shines brighter just for her to glow more
during the darkest hour
bathed in sunlight, the moon adores
the sun for their love thats
written in the stars

Sarah Cowan

Unrecognizable

when we first met, I was broken:
on the highest dose of antidepressants
terrible family problems
insecure of how I look
and I hurt myself to feel something

why would anyone love somebody like me?
I'm so broken

looking beyond my scars and hurt
you held me in your arms and supported me
helping me build myself back up
thinking on how my life is then and now
it is like night and day

happier, off my antidepressants completely,
I finally believe I am beautiful
and I have been clean for 4 years
because of you, I have learned to embrace
myself and cherish every stretch mark
every scar, and every aspect of everything
that makes me, *me*.

and you love me just as much as you have
since day one

Loving You

loving you was learning that love can come easy
love is learning that I am loveable
I know everyone always leaves me
you proved that true love lasts and that
any bump in the road is only a bump in the road

loving you was like a breath of fresh air
like all of my wounds are delicately tended for
all my needs are being taken care of

loving you was knowing that I found
someone who can love me wholeheartedly

Switch

I called him crying
life got too much and I told
myself I couldn't take it anymore

he told me it's okay and
helped me calm down
think logically and remind me
that it's all going to be okay

I don't know how he always does it
but we ended the call laughing

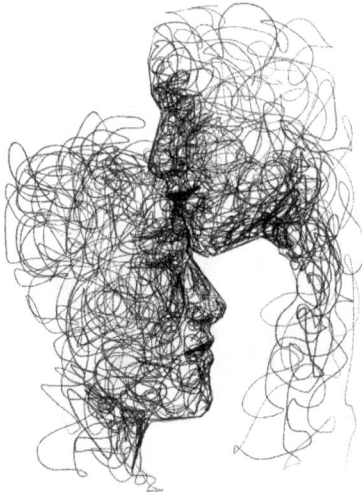

Lifetime

I will search for you in every lifetime
in another lifetime, we will be the two birds
flying high in the sky
the two flowers dancing in the breeze

in every lifetime, I will not
stop until I find you
over and over again

Clicked

I couldn't think we could get better
but we did.

we used to say, "see you next weekend,"
now I say
"see you after work"

we used to give each other a kiss at the door
then I'd fall asleep that night with a cold bedside
now I turn over and give you a loving kiss

it's like you fell more in love with
seeing my routine of life
yet also creating a new routine
together

now you finally caught a glimpse of
what the rest of our lives
could look like

and I wouldn't want it any other way

Want

I want you
every fiber of my being
I want you
I want our sunny days and cloudy nights
your best days and the worst days
I want you

the days when the world gets too tough
or the days your smile is shining brighter
than the sun above us
I want you

I want to dance stupidly in the kitchen while
we wait for our popcorn
I want to shower with you
I want to live my life with you
till we're old and wrinkly
right by my side, where you are meant to be

there isn't anyone I'd want to be with
but you

No Storms Last Forever

you may not believe me in this moment
but it is going to be okay

there are rainbows after the storm
sun after the clouds
a smile after the broken

this is a glimpse in time where maybe
things aren't in your control
let the highs and lows flow past you
and trust that
the rainbow will come after the rain because
no storms last forever

Last One

I want to be the last one to love you
maybe I'm not your first love
but I want to be your last

the last one to have inside jokes with you
the last one to know all of your flaws and
imperfections
the last one you bring home to meet your family

I want to be the one that you can call home
I don't want anyone else to take my spot
as I have given you my heart for hopefully
the final time in my life
and I hope you are doing the same

Beautifully Loved

as long as I'm alive and breathing

you will never feel nothing again
building you up from the ground
I will be your roof
protecting you from everything possible

you will never need to stare at the empty ceiling
and wonder if you are worth the air you breathe
for I will use all my air to keep you here

you will never have to feel unloved
as you lay your head to rest
I will be the one to remind you
how beautifully loved you are

Sit With It

people try to kiss a cigarette
to try and forget them
hug a bottle that makes them feel
warm and fuzzy on the inside
try and replace them to finally feel a warm body
in the same bed you two slept together in
do anything all the time to simply numb your brain
and stop feeling

don't

sit with it
deal with the emotions
a large part of healing is feeling everything
and learning to face the hurt, the sorrow, and the
pain
face it
don't run away from it

Never

I'm never going to forget you
no matter where we go in life
I am never going to forget you

I'm never going to forget your eyes
especially how they change to a different
shade of blue when we're in the shower
and you stare at me lovingly with water
dripping down your face

I'm never going to forget how
you can make me smile in one word
or can read me like a favourite book

I'll never forget the way you have touched my heart
caressed it gently, even on those hard days
loving me raw and staying here by my side

Five Years

5 and a half years
66 months
2008 days
48,180 hours
of loving you

I didn't see anyone else going through
love and life with me
I craved to have you on my side
you've seen me at my worst and
still loved me just the same
as for me at my best

I can't imagine what my life
would be like without you

I have loved you for so long
and I'll love you for many more

Help

I asked for help today
as a certified stranger stared at me
through a computer screen
I began to tell her what my problems were:
anxiety, depression, grief, anger . . .
and the list dragged on and on

as my first session concluded,
thoughts polluted my mind
my teenage, past self tapping me
on the shoulder
"thank you," she whispered to me
"there is no shame in asking for help
we needed this for many years"

it takes a lot for me to ask for help
I'm not strong enough if I break down
cause I have been known to
do it all myself without help.
I'm always the strong one

but I can't do this all alone
I need help
and there is no shame in asking

Not Her Story

her eyes gaze over their composition
relooking at all the fine details of it all:
the pressure of saying yes to being the girlfriend
the cheering crowd and blushing girl
after she said yes
the ugly parts of
having to beg for him to love her
fighting for him to stay
abandoning her and making her heal on her own

without him
without anyone

for a first true love
she never wanted it to be that way
she loved him
truly and genuinely
now she grew stronger from his absence
the girl who put everything on the line for him
just for him to walk away and not come back
leaving her wondering why he hurt her that way

after the thousandth time of rereading their
composition,
she couldn't realize that she did the best she could
the person she is now is different from
the one he once spoke to
she couldn't help but see that it is not her story
anymore

his affect and what he has done lives in her mind
but she knows that he did what he thought was right
she hopes with no malicious intent

they were only kids
how could they have known any better?

their story will live on with the memories
but that doesn't mean the heartbreak
will follow anymore

He Knows Me

how do I explain to everyone else
the way you perfectly love me?
how we just know and understand each other
without questioning whether
love truly is at the surface

our love goes beyond the surface
he knows me like my favourite book
while I know him like his favourite video game

how can I explain to someone else
how much I have poured my soul into you
our love is something I can't explain
something I'll never be able to justify
for everyone else

I stare at you with loving eyes
and relief knowing that no one
needs to know why my heart chose you

I love you because you make me feel whole
and nobody can take that away from me

Like A Leaf

with trembling hands
I turn the page to embrace the
change of the unknown

I am not feeling ready
but I know I can't stay here

in order to progress forward
I need to move forward and not stay here

I am meant to go far
travel and not stay stationary
not knowing what the future may hold
I still choose to turn over a new leaf
to know that it is for the better

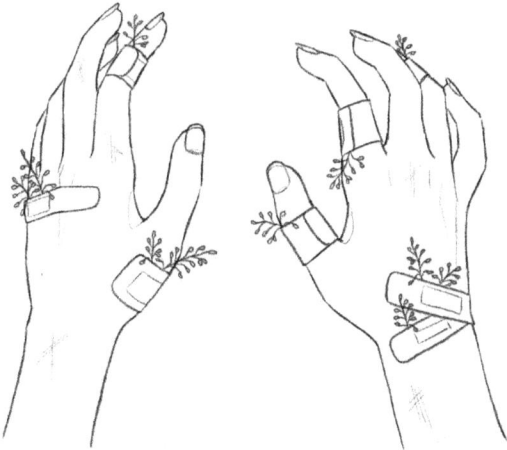

Life Goes On

when bad things happen
remember that life goes on
when the universe rips away who
you loved most, know that life goes on
the person who you loved realized
they don't love you anymore?
life goes on

can't be stuck reliving the past
because you won't be able see
what's ahead of you

turn off those blinders
mourn
cry
grieve the change but remember life goes on

people around you care and
will do anything to help you

Stop To Smell The Flowers

we never get a chance to slow down
never get a chance to stop
take this moment to look within

how do you feel?
are you happy with where you are?
if something is off, what is it?
can you pinpoint what makes you happy?
what about things you want to change?

healing begins when you look within yourself
and look up and smell the goodness that
surround you

Listen Closely

the universe constantly tells you to listen
you're always being fed the answers
to all the questions you have

slow your breathing
and listen to the song of the world

with a calm mind and clear thoughts
you'll be able to hear the wind of answers
the world gives you a million different
answers all at once
but it is your responsibility to simplify
all the voices that blur into one

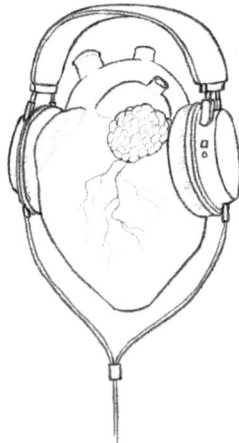

When I Feel Weak

when I feel too weak to keep going
I remind myself of the young girl
who was lost and on antidepressants
at the age of 15 and stayed on them for 6 years

who refused to eat, try strict diets
and weigh herself everyday
all because she hated her weight and
just wanted to fit into her stupid grad dress at 17

the kid who told herself that university isn't
for making friends, it's for learning
that she came home from school that first day
not have talked to a single soul

the teenager who was traumatized from
losing everything in a house fire
unsettled for years of loss and even
moved away from her small town
to escape her lingering past and trauma

I want all those versions of me to see
that it always was worth it to keep going

Vision

every so often, I like to close my eyes
see what my future has in store for me

I saw towering trees, forests that shower oxygen
around me with peace and quiet surrounding me
I felt the sun's warmth caressing
every inch of exposed skin
while the gentle wind cools me off.
I heard him laughing with his family
as he calls my name
wanting me to join the fun

I felt at home
I felt at peace

I look into my future and see a new life
a different place I now call home
a perspective I never saw coming
but it is something my soul urges me to make

this vision of mine brings euphoria
everything will be okay

Mirror

half a year has passed and
whenever I look in the mirror,
all I see is a girl who simply stopped crying

in the mirror, I still see someone who's grieving
she doesn't look as tired
her tears don't stain her cheeks anymore
but now she just cries once a week
rather than once a day

I see a woman who is still hurting
but I also see someone who still
manages to love life
even when the world made her miserable

I see a stronger woman
someone who isn't as fragile
as she was six months ago

Cabinet

I filled your cabinet today
four months from your passing
and I took the biggest
step in my healing journey

I had the thought with filling the space
with some fake flowers
tonight as I was alone writing poems
I felt the urge to make this step
I don't know if it was you
or if my own will power pushing me to do this

rising to my feet, I looked at my couple vases
of flowers I had scattered around my apartment
I saw some white flowers that were small enough
to fit in your cabinet

I knew those were the ones
picking up the vase, when I turned it around
I forgot it was the one I painted
long before your passing
I painted a smiling dog's face on it
it had your floppy ears

kneeling to the cabinet, I opened it and cried
staring at it empty, reminded me of how it was
yours
shakily placing the vase in your spot
it was no longer an eyesore to stare at

as I write this on my kitchen floor
it's like I could feel you with me in my kitchen
cheering for me on the other side
"I'm so proud of you Sarah, I love you."

I love you too. I did it.

The Cup

I didn't realize that I put something
in your cabinet today
I didn't even think about it
eight months since I emptied your cabinet
another four months of those flowers
occupying your spot

I have yet to move them

trying to clear up counter space
I grabbed an old water bottle of mine
and opened up your cabinet
as your white flowers and
painted puppy face stared back at me
I placed the bottle on the upper shelf of her cabinet
and closed it without a tear
without any hesitations

eight months ago, I couldn't dare open up the door
let alone put something of mine in there
ever so slowly
maybe this cabinet is becoming mine after all

Sarah Cowan

Never Really Gone

the pain of losing someone never truly goes away
my heart will still ache when I get
flashbacks of the day she passed away
or what it felt like to have her around again
the mourning never stops
you just get used to their absence
till it doesn't hurt anymore

but the pain will always live on
life goes on
with or without her
and she is the one that gets me out
of bed every morning
she's the one who hugs my heart
when it stings for a touch

Ladder To The Clouds

before me stands a ladder that goes
up to the clouds
where might this go?

climbing up the ladder, I am met with
a white picket fence, near a gate
I seem to be up in the clouds
like some sort of imaginary land
"there is someone who has been waiting for you"
I hear from behind me but nobody
was standing there
walking through the gate, I stood still
who has been waiting for me?

Ting Ting Ting

I know that sound
a dog tag rattling on a collar from movement
there she was
off in the distance, I saw my beloved fur baby
running to me through this field
of fluffy clouds and her wagging tail

dropping to my knees from shock
I watched my soul dog run to me
tears swelled in my eyes
her tail wagging happily

she was finally in my arms again
she is at home
sobs uncontrollably echoed in this haven
I couldn't let myself let her go

all this time, I've dreamed for her to come home
I miss her. and here she is before me
"Chewy," I sputtered, "I've missed you"
though she couldn't say anything back
I knew she has missed me just as much as
I have missed her
planting kisses on her head, and rubbing
my fingers between her fur
I hugged her tighter

I felt a hand place gently on my shoulder
with my soul dog still in my arms
I look up to find an older gentleman behind me
he looks like my mom

"she loves you greatly. and so do I
I've been taking good care of her"
I couldn't even get a word out
all I could do was go back to holding my dog
"we have to go now"
I held on tighter knowing I can't let her go again
that hand on my shoulder
squeezed me a bit tighter
"you'll find us in birds and dimes, my girl
we're always around you
Chewy's your little guardian angel"

I can feel a weight lift off me and
I found the courage to let her go
"I'll see you soon." I smile to Chewy
and I saw she smiled right back at me
"we'll see you soon, Sarah"
we exchange a tight hug
a new feeling of home

together my grandpa and Chewy
walked back into the sunlight
leaving me back at the ladder by the clouds

Christmas

today is Christmas day
day 228 of trying to heal from you
has it really been that long?
today marks my first true
holiday without you
and I *hate* it
I've never felt such melancholy
on a supposedly joyous day

I don't feel jolly and bright
there is a tugging in my heart
pulling me down into a deep sadness

"you should be here with me"
is what echos in my mind

"not up in heaven"

Without You

I have learned that life does not stop without you
if anything it actually began all over again
over time I began not to think of you as often
it's not that I forgot you
but it's the fact that healing allowed me to
still enjoy life even if it means without you

I lost myself at first without you
but as a sense of normal approaches
time heals all the open gashes to fine white lines
you are a moment in my past that I will never forget
I will continue to live without you

I won't stop smiling
I won't stop laughing
I will always think of you when I see a pretty sunset
or when I see a bird sitting on my balcony railing

my old life did stop when I lost you
but this new life has begun without you

February 24, 2025

when the clock struck midnight,
I held a moment of silence for you

for some weird reason, I felt obligated
to stay up till midnight
to watch as the clock struck twelve
just as if it was New Years
but today is your birthday
your first birthday in heaven

I long to give you a birthday hug
and a million kisses to tell you that I love you
instead I find myself stroking my computer
screen with the back of my finger
pretending that I'm petting your fur

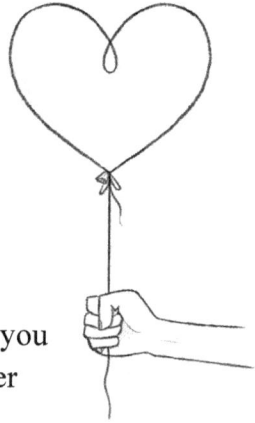

the first birthday without them is the worst
but all you can hope is that though their birthday
isn't celebrated as it was down here on earth
I pray that all our angels are loving you
and giving you the celebration you deserve

happy birthday, baby girl

May 11, 2025

today marks one year of your passing
a whole three hundred and sixty-five days
so much has changed since then
I wish I could tell you all about it

though your body is no longer here
there has never been a doubt in my mind
that you aren't watching over me consistently

I miss you every day
but one year ago, I was much worse
going through deep and heavy grief for the first
time
eventually finding healing in the chaos
I have learned to master the craft
and the art of beginning again

growth and death teaches you a lot
nothing is permanent
even when you think it is
life will make you begin all again
over and over and over

living in the present is truly
the best way to enjoy life

Sarah Cowan

mastering the art of beginning again
is a long and difficult journey
truly never ending
constant curveballs
constant change

but looking within yourself
has become such a fundamental
part in any healing,
not just grief

not only will you go through
all the emotions,
you will grow through them too

Closure

it's all over now
before you've known it
you have flipped all the pages
and are met with a blank one

"but I wasn't ready for it to end"
many will say, but endings are inevitable
even if you prepare for it
nothing ever compares to the real ending
any ending will ache but
what if I told you they never were to hurt?

Endings bring closure
maybe you don't see it, or maybe you never will
when one thing ends, another begins
a new life; a new adjustment

become hopeful for the future and remind your
heart
that this unstoppable ending doesn't mean forever
it just means that something better is on the next
page

Sarah Cowan

now that you've reached the end of this book
go start a new chapter in yours

INDEX OF TITLES

THE GENESIS..10

A LITTLE REMINDER..11

KNIFE AS WORDS...12

LOST...13

AND THIS IS HOW IT IS...................................14

PARALYZED..15

I DIDN'T HAVE A CHOICE................................16

SHE WAS ONLY A KID......................................18

DO YOU HEAR ME?..20

QUESTIONS & SILENCE...................................21

UNANSWERED QUESTIONS.............................22

PIECES OF YOU..24

WORDS...26

NOT LOVE...27

HE LOVES ME, HE LOVES ME NOT..............28

NOT AS PLANNED...30

BLINDSIDE..31

WHEN CHANGE COMES.................................32

IMPENDING DOOM...34

RAINBOW BRIDGE...36

RAW...38

IT'S BEEN ONE MONTH..................................39

UNFORGIVING...40

I LOST HER...41

NOT A BUG..42

REPLACEMENT..43

PAW PRINTED BLANKET................................44

I LOVE YOU..45

I MISS YOU...46

REGRET..47

SO HARD...48

AFTERMATH..49

I'M NOT READY...50

EMPTY...51

SHE'S DEAD...52

GRIEF WITH GRACE.......................................54

YOU WERE HERE..55

NOT THE SAME..56

FIRST TIME..57

ME VS THE WORLD..58

TIME PASSES..59

PICTURE IMPERFECT......................................60

GRIEF...61

SHOCKED..62

DEPRESSION..63

BETTER OFF DEAD....................................64

EMOTIONALLY UNSTABLE.........................68

STINGING SILVER.....................................69

CUT OFF...70

LET THEM...71

FIRST...72

RUN AWAY..73

UNREQUITED LOVE...................................74

NOT LIKE SHE USED TO............................75

FRESHEST AIR..76

TOO MUCH...77

STRENGTH...78

CASTLE..79

STILL STANDING.................................80

BACK THEN.....................................81

THE RUG.......................................82

IT'S NOT YOUR FAULT...........................83

IRREPLACEABLE.................................84

TATTOO..85

HABIT...86

READY...87

ENDURING LOVE.................................88

IT DOESN'T HURT LIKE IT DID...................89

ONWARD..90

DEATH...91

SEE YOU LATER.................................92

PETALS NOT THORNS.............................93

ECHOES OF YOUR PRESENCE.......................94

DO YOU SEE ME?...95

ECHOES OF PAWS...96

WHISPERS OF THE HEART...............................97

HEALING IN SILENCE......................................98

POEM AND THE POET.....................................99

GARDEN OF MEMORIES................................100

NUMB..102

FLASHBACK..103

TALK TO ME..104

NEW YEAR...105

PAW PRINTS FROM HEAVEN.......................106

KEEP SHINING...110

OVERFLOWING CUP.....................................111

SCIENCE..112

SENSITIVE SOULS...113

THOUSAND WAYS..114

FREE..115

NAKED..116

USED TO BE..117

WAS IT ME?..118

WHAT'S WORSE?..119

I AM 120

ODE TO SELF..121

YEARS..122

HEALING..123

SOUL GARDEN...124

HURT ME..125

MAGNETIC PULL...126

FORGET..127

PARALLEL UNIVERSE......................................128

RAINBOW..129

FOR THE PEOPLE.....................................130

GIFT OF TIME...131

FINAL WALK...132

I'M SORRY...133

DREAM...134

LIFE AFTER DEATH.................................135

REBRAND..136

LESSON..137

2:34PM...138

BAD DAYS..139

SLOW AND STEADY................................140

X MARKS THE SPOT...............................141

DEAD END..142

I SEE NOW...143

SOUL DOG..144

GONE..145

JUXTAPOSITION...146

SPINNING CIRCLES....................................147

MAY 11TH...148

TOGETHER AGAIN....................................149

LOVE & LOSS..150

INVISIBLE STRING....................................154

US 156

GIVING...158

WE JUST FIT...159

CALM...160

INSERT THEIR NAME HERE.....................161

IMAGINE...162

AS ONE...164

UNRECOGNIZABLE.................................165

LOVING YOU.......................................166

SWITCH..167

LIFETIME..168

CLICKED...169

WANT 170

NO STORMS LAST FOREVER......................171

LAST ONE..172

BEAUTIFULLY LOVED..............................173

SIT WITH IT..174

NEVER...175

FIVE YEARS..176

HELP 177

NOT HER STORY...................................178

HE KNOWS ME.....................................180

LIKE A LEAF...181

LIFE GOES ON..182

STOP TO SMELL THE FLOWERS.................183

LISTEN CLOSELY.......................................184

WHEN I FEEL WEAK..................................185

VISION...186

MIRROR...187

CABINET..188

THE CUP..190

NEVER REALLY GONE................................191

LADDER TO THE CLOUDS 192

CHRISTMAS 195

WITHOUT YOU...196

FEBRUARY 24, 2025...................................197

MAY 11, 2025...198

CLOSURE...200

About The Author

Sarah Cowan was born and raised in a small town in Alberta, Canada. If she isn't writing poetry, she can be found either writing a gatekept romance novel or listening to her favourite music. Publishing her first book in 2023, *Keep Me Sane*, charted top 3 on Amazon Canada's Hot New Releases in Love Poems and #6 in New Releases in Canadian Poetry. Since then she has been keeping busy by blogging and working on her next masterpiece. Sarah also studied at Concordia University of Edmonton and earned a Bachelor of Arts degree with a major in English.

More information and her blog can be found at www.sarahcowan.ca

www.ingramcontent.com/pod-product-compliance
Lightning Source LLC
Chambersburg PA
CBHW071426090426
42737CB00011B/1584